By Ed Masessa

SCHOLASTIC INC.
New York Toronto London Sydney
Auckland Mexico City New Delhi Hong Kong

Front Cover:
Background: ©Studio DMM Photography, Designs & Art/Shutterstock, © astudio/Shutterstock, © Albert Campbell/Shutterstock, © Albert Campbell/Shutterstock

Postcards: (clockwise) © Eric Isselée/Shutterstock, © Samot/Shutterstock, © Route66/Shutterstock, © Route66/Shutterstock, © Eric Isselée/Shutterstock, © Alexander Chaikin/Shutterstock, © iStockphoto, © Utekhina Anna/Shutterstock, © Atlaspix/Shutterstock

Back Cover: © yamix/Shutterstock

Interior:
All stamp backgrounds: © Studio DMM Photography, Designs & Art/Shutterstock, © astudio/Shutterstock, © Albert Campbell/Shutterstock, © Albert Campbell/Shutterstock
All dog bones: © Juampi Rodriguez/Shutterstock

Title page: © rtguest/Shutterstock; p. 3: © yamix/Shutterstock, © James Thew/Shutterstock; p. 4-5: (left to right) © Oxlock/Shutterstock, © iStockphoto, © iStockphoto, © sjgh/Shutterstock; p. 6-7: (left to right) © Fotogroove/Shutterstock, © Kamira/Shutterstock, © Dorottya Mathe/Shutterstock, © Galinapremiere/Shutterstock; p. 8-9: (left to right) © ShEd Artworks/Shutterstock, © megastocker/Shutterstock, © Kelly Richardson/Shutterstock, © megastocker/Shutterstock; p. 10-11: (left to right) © Atlaspix/Shutterstock, © Sverlova Mariya/Shutterstock , © Eric Isselée/Shutterstock, © Albert Campbell/Shutterstock; p. 12-13: (left to right) © Albert Campbell/Shutterstock, © iStockphoto, © Utekhina Anna/Shutterstock; p. 14-15: (left to right) © pdesign/Shutterstock, © Zoe Funnell/Shutterstock, © Lars Christensen/Shutterstock, © ShEd Artworks/Shutterstock, © Atlaspix/Shutterstock; p. 16-17: (left to right) © Albert Campbell/Shutterstock, © Worakit Sirijinda/Shutterstock, © Sergey Lavrentev/Shutterstock, © Route66/Shutterstock; p. 18-19: (left to right) © Alexander Chaikin/Shutterstock, © Eric Isselée/Shutterstock; p. 20-21: (left to right) © ShEd Artworks/Shutterstock, © Eric Isselée /Shutterstock, © Samot/Shutterstock, © Route66/Shutterstock; p. 22-23: (left to right) © granata1111/Shutterstock, © Demid Borodin/Shutterstock, © Hannamariah/Shutterstock, © ShEd Artworks/Shutterstock; p. 24-25: (left to right) © Georgescu Gabriel/Shutterstock, © Utekhina Anna/Shutterstock, © Route66/Shutterstock, © ShEd Artworks/Shutterstock; p. 26-27: (left to right) © Robyn Mackenzie/Shutterstock, © BlankaB/Shutterstock, © Andreas Gradin/Shutterstock, © Albert Campbell/Shutterstock; p. 28-29: (left to right) © Albert Campbell/Shutterstock, © chrisdouglas123/Shutterstock, © Eric Isselée/Shutterstock, © helen von allmen/Shutterstock; p. 30-31: (left to right) © ekler/Shutterstock, © Izmael/Shutterstock, © Andrey Perminov/Shutterstock, © Albert Campbell/Shutterstock; p. 32: © gabor2100/Shutterstock

ISBN 978-0-545-38558-9

10 9 8 7 6 5 4 3 2 12 13 14 15 16 17/0
Printed in the U.S.A 40

First printing, January 2012

Dogs come in many shapes and sizes. Some are so small they could fit in your pocket and travel with you wherever you go.

Although they come from different places, all these pups would love to be your friend. So get ready to meet these travel-size pups as you take a trip around the world!

Boston Terrier

This pup was truly "made in America," when a group of people in Boston crossed an English Terrie with a Bulldog in the 1860s.

The Boston Terrier is nicknamed "the American Gentleman." However, it is very strong for its siz and will not back down in a fight.

Havanese

The Havanese (have-a-knees) is a playful dog that has a great sense of humor. It loves doing silly tricks. This made it a favorite pet among Cuban plantation owners.

It is very smart, can learn tricks quickly, and was often trained to perform in circuses!

Chihuahua

The Chihuahua (chi-wow-wa) is named after the state of Chihuahua, Mexico, where it was discovered. It is the world's smallest dog breed. Chihuahuas are so small that some people carry them in their pockets or purses. Despite their size, they can be very good watchdogs.

SALIDA

Cavalier King Charles Spaniel

This tiny spaniel was named after King Charles II, who was known as the Cavalier King. Most owners call it the Cav. Just like bigger spaniels, it likes to chase birds.

The Cav has a sweet face and long, bushy ears that almost look like ponytails.

Height:
12–13 inches tall

Weight:
13–18 pounds

Originally from:
England

Yorkshire Terrier

Known as the Yorkie, this is a big dog in a small package. In its native land of England, it was used to hunt rats and mice. It also makes an excellent alarm dog.

Its long, silky coat has a natural part right down the center of its back.

Height:
8–9 inches tall

Weight:
under 7 pounds

Originally from:
England

Cairn Terrier

This feisty little guy loves to chase squirrels and other small animals. Many years ago it was trained to do just that—chase rodents out of rock piles called cairns. And it also makes a very good watchdog.

The most famous Cairn Terrier is Toto from the 1939 movie *The Wizard of Oz.*

Papillon

The word *papillon* (pappy-on) is French for "butterfly." Look at its face and you can see where the Papillon gets its name from—its upright ears look just like the wings of a butterfly! It was very popular among the kings' courts in France.

Height:
8–11 inches tall

Weight:
5–10 pounds

Originally from:
France

French Bulldog

Think of the French Bulldog as the funny younger brother of the English Bulldog. Not only is it smaller, but it has "bat ears" that make it look smart and alert—which it is!

These dogs became very popular in France because women thought they were clever and cuddly with a good sense of humor.

Bolognese

This puppy takes its name from the Italian city of Bologna. Hundreds of years ago, noblemen of Italy would give these pups as gifts to visiting kings and queens.

While it is just as cute as the Havanese, the Bolognese (bowl-owe-knees) breed is harder to find in the United States.

Height:
9–12 inches tall

Weight:
5–8 pounds

Originally from:
Bologna, Italy

Miniature Dachshund

The name *dachshund* (daks-hund) means "badger dog" in German. With its short legs and long body, the Dachshund could crawl into badger holes and flush badgers out. But the miniature breed is more likely to chase rabbits and squirrels.

Height:
5–8 inches tall

Weight:
under 11 pounds

Originally from:
Germany

Italian Greyhound

Don't let their name fool you. Italian Greyhounds are actually from Greece. They got their names because Italian royalty loved having these elegant dogs as pets. Pictures of dogs that look like this one appear on the tombs of ancient mummies!

Height:
13–15 inches tall

Weight:
7–15 pounds

Originally from:
Greece

SALIDA
CYPRUS

NEXT
35 km

Australian Terrier

This little ball of energy is a hunter and a digger. It is the national Terrier of Australia, where it is used to hunt snakes, rats, mice, and other pests.

Also known as the Blue and Tan, it is a workaholic that is used for guarding cattle and sheep.

Pug

Pug might be short for *pugnus* which means “fist” in Latin. A Pug’s round face is full of wrinkles and looks like a clenched fist. So it is the perfect name for the dog.

Some think the Pug was bred by monks in Tibet to be an entertainer.

Height:
about 10 inches tall

Weight:
14–18 pounds

Originally from:
Tibet

SALIDA

TRAVEL-SIZE PUPS

Around the World

SCHOLASTIC READER LEVEL 2 250-750 WORDS

By Ed Masessa

SCHOLASTIC

This book belongs to:
Avery
Grosse

Japanese Chin

When you see a Japanese Chin, you might think of feathers. The dog has a long, silky coat, so its ears, legs, tail, and neck seem to be layered with feathers.

Originally from China, they became the favorite pets of ancient Japanese emperors and were bred to be loving lapdogs.

Height:
8–11 inches tall

Weight:
5–10 pounds

Originally from:
China

Pups Around the World

Chihuahua
MEXICO

Havanese
CUBA

Cairn Terrier
SCOTLAND

Dachshund
GERMANY

Boston Terrier
USA

Italian Greyhoun
GREECE

Charles Spaniel
ENGLAND

French Bulldog
FRANCE

Pug
TIBET

Japanese Chin
CHINA

Bolognese
ITALY

Australian Terrie
AUSTRALIA